Rolling Homes

Rolling Homes

Handmade Houses on Wheels

Jane Lidz

A & W Visual Library
New York

Published by
A & W Publishers, Inc.
95 Madison Avenue
New York, New York 10016

Library of Congress Catalog Card Number: 78-72506

ISBN: 0-89104-128-1 (HC)
ISBN: 0-89104-129-x (PB)

Designed by David Charlsen

Printed in the United States of America

With the spirit of yesterday's covered wagon and the mobility of today's recreational vehicle, these individually crafted houses on wheels form an original artistic and cultural movement. They combine the do-it-yourself tradition with the American faith that "you can take it with you." Blending art with technology and economy with style, they satisfy the desire for freedom, simplicity and self-expression.

To the housetruckers, who are the life of this book.

Very special thanks to Jerry;
also to Alan Boner, Tom Jacobs, John Reynolds and
everyone else in the Department of Architecture,
University of Oregon, who helped me keep the book rolling.

Contents

More than just old trucks and buses that provide low-cost housing, these rolling homes are designed and built by people who want the option of combining home, work and travel.

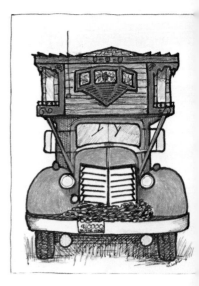

Most of the vehicles in this book have been through many changes—
in ownership, function, color and mechanical parts—but their original
body style remains unchanged. Fenders, grills and bumpers are like
friendly faces from the past.

The "housetruckers" have gained a special self-confidence and pride by having done it themselves. Each rolling home is a personal solution to a difficult problem: how to design a home in a rectangular space no larger than 8 ft. wide, 40 ft. long and 13½ ft. high. The largest housetrucks are comparable in size to a large living room (about 300 sq. ft.); the smallest are comparable to a pantry (36 sq. ft.).

Saving space is the basis for two unwritten laws of living in a housetruck:

If it isn't useful, you don't need it.

If it doesn't fit in the truck, you can't have it.

Most nooks and crannies have built-in storage space and each home has at least one secret hiding place for valuables.

A rolling home can be reoriented for optimum light, shade, heat and ventilation. Windows at many levels provide a variety of views of the outside, and abundant light creates a feeling of spaciousness. With the contrast of high and low, large and small, and public and private places, one room has the advantages of many. The most successful designs are multipurpose: drawing a curtain makes a room, removing a crib's side rails makes a couch, lowering a tailgate makes a porch.

Many of the fixtures are antiques: ornate wood- and gas-burning stoves, oak ice chests and kerosene lamps that have been restored to their original usefulness. The housetruckers build with materials they find at garage sales, flea markets, estate auctions, secondhand stores and demolition sites. Recycling materials decreases the cost of remodeling and increases the variety and character of their homes. Old and new objects, romantic and practical approaches combine to create a patchwork effect that recalls memories of the past and enriches fantasies of future adventures on the road.

The individual owners attach varying importance to mobility, space, light, privacy, convenience and cost. These factors help determine the vehicle and design which best fit their owners' needs and desires—school bus, delivery van or log truck.

Buses

Buses have a distinctive form that is not found on a flatbed truck. The shell is convenient as a temporary shelter, but converting a bus into a comfortable, spacious and well-lit house usually means raising the roof.

With no previous building experience, Jonathan began remodeling his school bus with some help from his friends. A welder raised the roof, and Jonathan claims the rest was common sense. Skylights admit plenty of light and leave enough wall space for artistic displays. The banks of bus windows are well-positioned for cross ventilation and allow the sun to heat the bus.

As owner, designer, builder and curator, Jonathan transformed an ordinary bus into a showplace for his collection of antiques and kitsch known as "The American Institute of Obnoxious Art." Jonathan is a member of the Northwest Touring Company, a community of craftspeople who travel together to fairs and share ideas, information and skills.

1. *Facing front.*

2. *Facing back.*

   Since there is no separate driving cab, a bus has more continuous interior space than a truck with the same exterior dimensions.

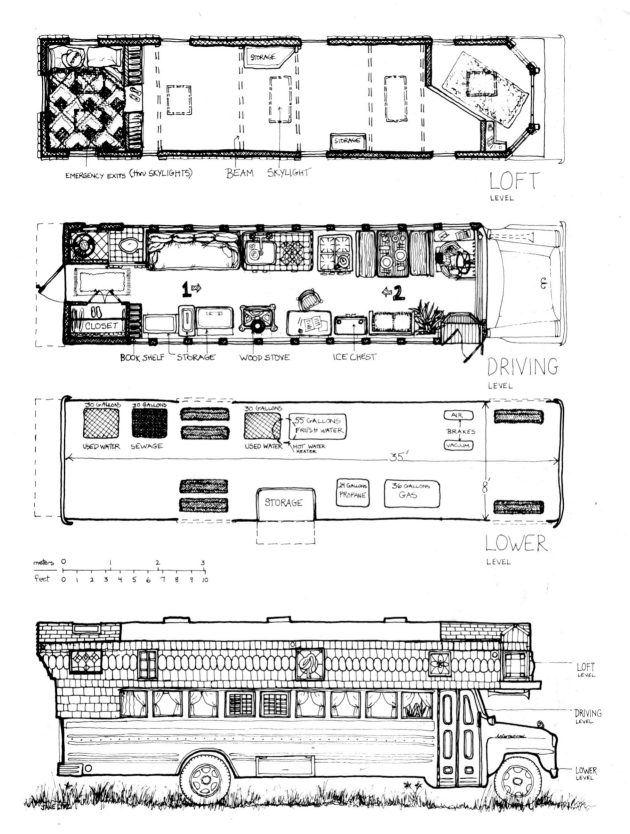

EMERGENCY EXITS (thru SKYLIGHTS)   BEAM   SKYLIGHT

STORAGE

STORAGE

LOFT
LEVEL

CLOSET

1 ⇨   ⇦ 2

BOOK SHELF   STORAGE   WOOD STOVE   ICE CHEST

DRIVING
LEVEL

30 GALLONS   30 GALLONS   30 GALLONS

55 GALLONS
FRESH WATER

AIR
BRAKES
VACUUM

USED WATER   SEWAGE   USED WATER   HOT WATER
HEATER

35'

8'

STORAGE

24 GALLONS
PROPANE

36 GALLONS
GAS

LOWER
LEVEL

meters 0   1   2   3
feet 0 1 2 3 4 5 6 7 8 9 10

LOFT
LEVEL

DRIVING
LEVEL

LOWER
LEVEL

JANE LIDZ

15

Utilities

Sink brass marine fixtures, Spanish tile counter top

Shower antique brass, hotel shower ring

Toilet chemical flush

Light kerosene lamps, candles, battery-operated (12 v.)

Heat wood-burning stove, "Cheerful" model, 1910

Cooking propane stove, "Reliable" model, 1907

Refrigeration antique oak ice chest

"My stove is a gas
and it's semi-reliable."

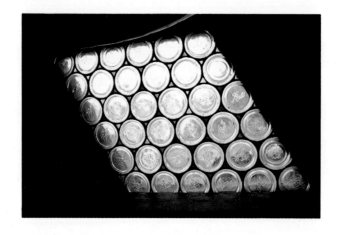

Facts and Figures

Model   '58 International school bus

Purchase date/cost   '75 / $900

Remodel time/cost   '75—'77 / $7,500

Miles per gallon   4—5

Weight   19,000 lbs. (8,618.4 kg.)—(actual)

Exterior dimensions   12'6" (3.84 m.)—height
35' (10.66 m.)—length
8' (2.43 m.)—width

Interior space   225 sq. ft. (20.9 sq. m.)—driving level
76 sq. ft. (7.06 sq. m.)—loft level

Materials, exterior   cedar, steel and glass
interior   cedar, oak, redwood, walnut and brass

Past use   66-passenger school bus

Present use   home for 1 adult; Art Gallery

Nicknames   "Winnebagel," "Obscene-a-Cruiser"

"It's both a bus and a fantasy."

There's more than one way to raise the roof.

Even if they don't have to worry about housing shortages, house-truckers still must find a place to park. (The same legal restrictions apply to housetrucks and motorhomes.) Occasionally they park in campgrounds and trailer parks, but usually the vehicles are tucked away in residential driveways, backyards, or at the end of country roads.

Function follows form when the bus entrance becomes a part-time shower stall.

(See Cost/Time, page 77.)

Logan and Debby use their back porch to store skis, bicycles and other equipment. It converts into a sitting porch when the tailgate is lowered and a platform is placed over the poles.

Logan spent several weeks peeling and varnishing these fir poles. To warm the color of the wood, he turned them in the sun several times each day.

"I drove an old school bus home and surprised Phyllis with it as a Christmas present. She about fell over."

Like other housetruckers, E.B. and Phyllis kept the cost down by using scrap materials and doing all the work themselves. They learned as they went along, taking classes in everything from upholstery to wiring and plumbing. "Nothing was impossible as long as we were willing to do it three or four times to get it right."

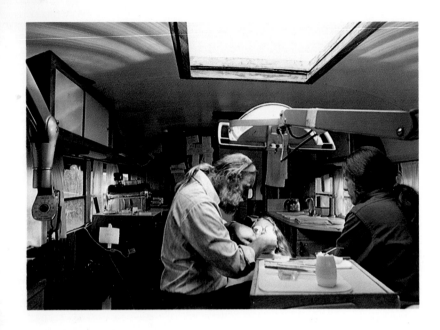

With his office in a '49 Diamond-T bus, this dentist can serve several rural communities.

In the springtime, "Doc" likes to park under a flowering tree, making the view through the open skylight a pleasant surprise for his patients.

Many craftspeople work, sell and advertise from their rolling homes. As one housetrucker said, "You can sell anything you want 'cause you've got the best billboard in town."

Stones mark the path to this backyard bus which used to be a home
and is now a mail-order herb office and "guest" bus.

This '48 Dodge bus sports a roof graft from a '62 VW, two airplane cockpit canopies, a solar-heated oven (below the octagon), indoor and outdoor showers and a sauna.

"Patches" is home and studio for its leathersmith/feathersmith/jeweler/gem-cutter owner, Silverbear.

(See Cost/Time, page 77.)

40

The loft within a loft in this '48 International school bus was completed by the baby's father just before her birth in her parents' bed.

Small Rigs

The smaller the vehicle, the more mobile it is. Small rigs consume less gasoline, are easier to drive and park, and have better access to out-of-the-way camping spots.

Most of their owners are single, but as one housetrucker said, "They're also good for two in love or eight in fun."

"Patience," a remodeled delivery truck, houses Joan, Willie and their dog, Jasmine, in a very small space.

In the past 30 years, Patience has been through several reincarnations: a New York milk truck, a plumber's tool truck and a housetruck for four different owners in the last 14 years.

Joan and Willie find that the essentials for traveling are maps, matches, water, shovel, toilet paper and extra fuel. They enjoy forming caravans with other housetruckers or bringing their house with them to visit friends and family. At home base they park on their land in the country.

The side awning folds out to create a sheltered porch-like space,
making any place their backyard.

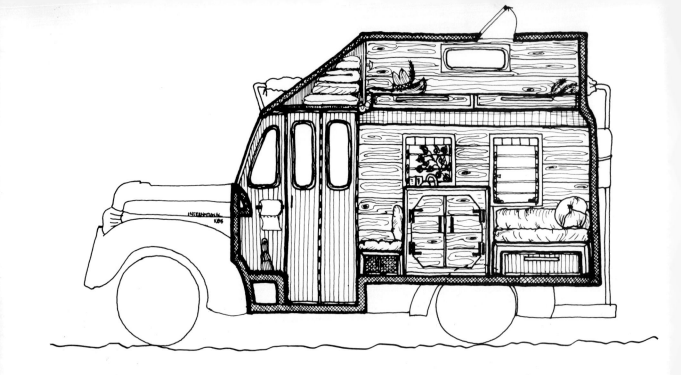

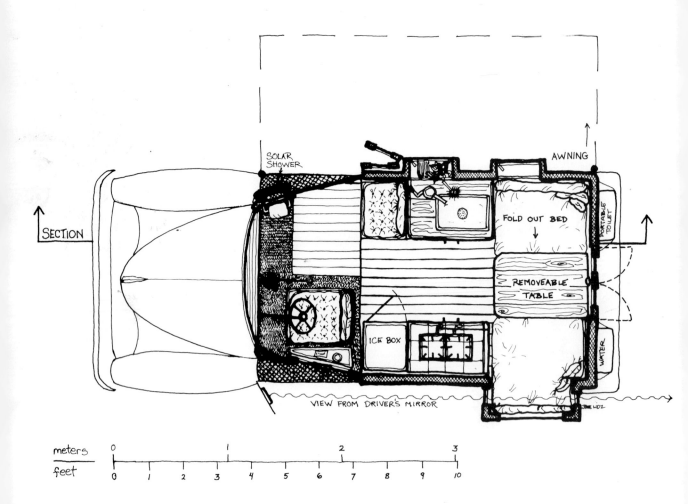

SOLAR
SHOWER

AWNING

SECTION

PORTABLE
TOILET

FOLD OUT BED

REMOVEABLE
TABLE

WATER

ICE BOX

VIEW FROM DRIVER'S MIRROR

meters	0			1			2			3
feet	0	1	2	3	4	5	6	7	8	9	10

Utilities

Sink   forced air pump, 10 gallons (37.8 l.) fresh water piped from outside tank

Shower   solar-heated, 2½-gallon (9.46 l.) black plastic water bag with nozzle

Toilet   portable toilet, shovel

Light   propane, kerosene lamps

Heat   propane stove, car heater, or "boiling a pot of water"

Cooking   2-burner wrought-iron propane stove

Refrigeration   ice-box

Facts and Figures

Model   '49 International delivery van

Purchase date/cost   '77 / traded '59 pick-up

Remodel time/cost   4 months / $1,500

Miles per gallon   10

Weight   6,400 lbs. (2,899.2 kg.)—(actual)

Exterior dimensions   9' (2.74 m.)—height
15'6" (4.75 m.)—length
6' (1.82 m.)—width

Interior space   55 sq. ft. (5.10 sq. m.)

Materials, exterior   redwood, steel
interior   knotty pine, redwood, fir

"Patience is slow, but you're going in style."

(See Cost/Time, page 77.)

50

Pam built "Mañana" to ride on her '52 Dodge pick-up. Design inspiration for the 6' x 6½' convertible cottage came from doll houses and canvas tents as well as gypsy and Conestoga wagons.

(See Cost/Time, page 77.)

56

57

58

Trucks

There are fewer design constraints in building a home on a flatbed truck since there is no shell to remodel and the driving compartment is separate from the living area. The house/cab division allows people the option of building their home on the truck bed and removing it if they want to. A large truck makes a good base for a rolling home because it is made to carry heavy loads and travel long distances. Michael's log truck with its 10 wheels, 15 gears and powerful engine can cruise at 55 mph all day.

Michael began building his home on the truck bed after apprenticing to a carpenter who had converted a school bus into a rolling home. He parks his house in the country on land he rents in exchange for his labor. Finding carpentry jobs is easy because his home is a mobile display of his craftsmanship. Michael also works closely with other housetruckers in an informal owner/builder network. His cabinets and stained-glass windows appear in many of his friends' homes as well as in his own.

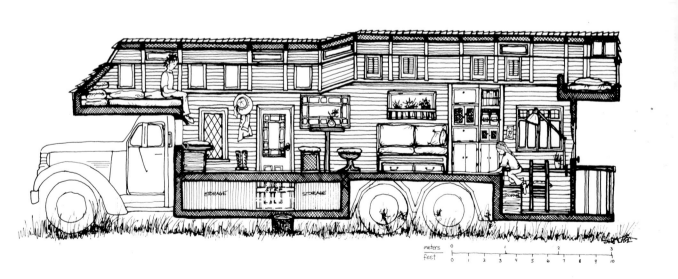

61

"As an artist I wanted to create an inspiring and supportive place to draw or play music. Redwood, cedar and skylights make me feel great."

When his son was born, Michael's studio space became the baby's bedroom and the drafting desk became a crib. In a few years the loft over the back porch will be the child's bedroom, and the crib will be a couch.

Facts and Figures

Model   '48 International log truck

Purchase date/cost   '75 / $500

Construction time/cost   1½ years / $2,500;
"liveable in 4 months, but not finished yet."

Miles per gallon   5

Weight   30,000 lbs. (13,600 kg.)—(actual)

Exterior dimensions   12′6″ (3.84 m.)—height
36′6″ (11.15 m.)—length
8′   (2.4 m.)—width

Interior space   150 sq. ft. (13.93 sq. m.)—driving level
55 sq. ft. (5.10 sq. m.)—loft level
33 sq. ft. (3.06 sq. m.)—lower level

Materials, exterior   cedar siding and shingles, bus windows for
skylights
interior   cedar walls, redwood beams, oak floor

Past use   log truck, water truck

Present use   home—2 adults, 1 child

Utilities

Sink   double sink with hand pump, 60-gallon (227.1 l.) fresh-water holding tank

Shower   bucket above pack porch

Toilet   portable toilet

Light   kerosene, candles, electric

Heat   cast-iron Swedish wood-burning stove, portable electric heater

Cooking   antique propane stove, "Detroit Jewel," 1928

Refrigeration   ice chest

(See Cost/Time, page 77.)

The bay window was originally built as a nursery for a baby and is now a nursery for 50 plants.

Cost/Construction

Many housetruckers find that living in a vehicle is the least expensive way to own a home. Comparing costs with conventional housing is difficult because labor is not included in the cost of an owner-built rolling home. However, the capital investment and maintenance costs are much less than for a stationary home.

Even though most housetruckers consume less energy than a conventional family with a house and car, they have chosen a life-style fueled by gasoline. In search of a better alternative, some have converted their vehicles to run on propane or methane.

"Gas is my rent."

PURCHASE   CONSTRUCTION   TOTAL

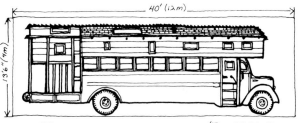

$ 1,600. $ 3,500. $ 5,100.

Date: '71   Time: 5 yrs.

page 25   '57 INTERNATIONAL

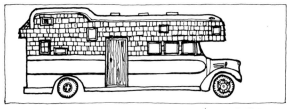

$ 750. $ 2,500. $ 3,250.

Date: '75   Time: 3 yrs.

page 40   '48 INTERNATIONAL

$ 500. $ 500. $ 1,000.

Date: '77   Time: 3 mos.

page 50   '52 DODGE

$ 175. $ 1,025. $ 1,200.

Date: '72   Time: 9 mos.

page 56   '48 DODGE

$ 600. $ 6,000. $ 6,600.

Date: '72   Time: 3 yrs.

page 68   '51 FEDERAL

$ 1,500. $10,000. $11,500.

Date: '75   Time: 2 yrs.

page 84   '59 INTERNATIONAL

NOTE: All figures are approximate.
      Cost does not include trades, bargains, luck and labor.
      Time does not include number of hours or people.

Raising the roof is the major construction job in converting a bus into
a home. The bus can be cut above the windows, below the windows,
or both.

The whole body can be removed, leaving only the chassis and no clue that it was once a bus.

To accommodate a growing family, this '50 Dodge school bus is being remodeled for the third time in eight years.

On the back of this '59 International diesel log truck is a rolling home "framed just like a house." This was the construction sequence:

- cut and extended frame of truck
- built flatbed on frame
- framed walls on flatbed and lifted them into position
- covered walls with plywood and tar paper
- installed —open truss beams (clear fir)
    —roof (shingles—knotty pine ceiling)
    —window casings (clear fir)
    —siding (beveled cedar and scalloped shingles)
    —plumbing and electrical wiring
    —windows and doors
    —interior insulation (fiberglass)
    —paneling (tongue-and-groove cedar)
    —built-in cabinets (oak), couch (mahogany)
    —floor (oak)
    —furniture

(See Cost/Time, page 77.)

"We designed our house around the windows."

Glen placed a fan-shaped beveled glass window in the same position it had held in his last housetruck. After eight years of living in three different vehicles, Glen and Nancy gathered many ideas and materials for their ultimate housetruck.

Housetrucks must be built to withstand the rigors of the road. Screws, nuts and bolts, ring shank nails and glue are used in construction. Glen rebuilt all his beveled and stained-glass windows with zinc to stiffen them for traveling.

"If you're really into it, you're never finished."

Jane Pincus Lidz has lived in New York, Colorado, Wisconsin and Oregon with her husband, Jerry, and her dog, Zak. After graduation from Sarah Lawrence College she taught art, studied film, and worked as a film animator and professional photographer. Currently, she is a graduate teaching fellow in Architecture at the University of Oregon.